Evening Wine

Drawings by

GLEN G. GREENWALT

HarperCollins books may be purchased for educational, business, or sales promotional use. For information please write: Special Markets Department, HarperCollins Publishers. 10 East 53rd Street, New York, NY 10022.

Book design by Kathleen A. Servidio

ISBN: 9781883285548

12 13 14 15 16 SCP 10 9 8 7 6 5 4 3 2 1

Messages in the Bottle

Every bottle of wine contains a whole world of meaning.

To the attentive drinker, a fine wine speaks about the place it comes from, the grapes it is made from and the weather that nurtured it. Beyond that, it reflects an era's culture and taste. And as it ages, it offers insight into its joys and its complexities.

Great thinkers through the ages have understood these messages in the bottle, and many have celebrated wine and the pleasures it brings. This book ranges far and wide to find the most concise, insightful and telling "tasting notes" about the pleasures of wine. There are passages from the Bible, proverbs from China and jokes from W.C Field. Poets and philosophers have their say. Above all, there is Shakespeare, who celebrated wine in so many of his famous plays.

We enjoy wine as a sensory pleasure, as an aesthetic experience and as an aid to good health and happiness. This engaging book deepens the experience with thought-provoking aphorisms and delightful illustrations. Pour a glass, and enjoy.

— Marvin R. Shanken,
Editor and Publisher, *Wine Spectator*

Author's Note

The drawings in the three-book series — *Morning Coffee, Afternoon Tea*, and *Evening Wine* — grew out of my observations of people who come together to swap stories with friends, laugh, debate politics, interview for a job, read the paper or a book, or simply stare out of the window.

I have taught college religion and philosophy, but in my forties, at the encouragement of a colleague, I purchased a sketchbook. Drawing provided me a way of observing life with greater care than my own casual observations or academic studies had ever disclosed. At fifty-five, I finished a graduate degree in figurative studies.

I could draw a perfect likeness of a model holding a pose over several hours, but to learn how to draw people in motion, I began sketching in my local New York City coffee shop. Later, I moved out west, where I added several tea houses and a bistro to my favorite places to draw.

At first, I would hide the fact that I was drawing people. But they always noticed, and almost without exception, they were flattered, often adjusting their clothing or hair. If anyone appeared uncomfortable, or too posed, I would move on. I simply wanted to capture the everyday moments of life that usually go unobserved, to record how tea, coffee, and wine are the lubricants of social interaction, or of sweet solitude.

These books are a celebration of shared moments in our lives through my pen and ink — accompanied by the words of wiser people than I.

Glen Greenwalt, Seattle, 2012

Give me books, French wine, fruit,
fine weather, and a little music played out
of doors by someone I do not know.

JOHN KEATS

glen greenwalt
2009

Wine is constant proof that God loves us
and loves to see us happy.

BENJAMIN FRANKLIN

gley greenwalt
2009

A man not old, but mellow, like good wine.

STEPHEN PHILLIPS

LE PICHET

Hours

No Smoking
Smoking is Prohibited!

glen greenwalt
2009

In water one sees one's own face;
but in wine, one beholds the
heart of another.

OLD FRENCH PROVERB

glen greenwalt
2009

Forsake not an old friend;
for the new is not comparable to him:
A new friend is as new wine;
when it is old, thou shalt drink
it with pleasure.

ECCLESIASTICUS 9:10

glen greenwalt
2009

Men are like wine—
Some turn to vinegar,
but the best improve with age.

POPE JOHN XXIII

glen greenwalt
2011

A man cannot make him laugh—
but that's no marvel; he drinks no wine.

WILLIAM SHAKESPEARE

Roc Bleu
Epoisses
Ste Maure
Brillat Savarin

frites

plats du jour

glen greenwalt
2009

Give me wine to wash me clean
of the weather-stains of care.

Ralph Waldo Emerson

glen greenwalt
2006

There is not the hundredth part of wine consumed in this kingdom that there ought to be. Our foggy climate wants help.

JANE AUSTEN

glen greenwalt
2009

The wine cup is the silver well, where truth,
if truth there be, doth dwell.

WILLIAM SHAKESPEARE

glen glerawalt
2011

How simple and frugal a thing is happiness:
A glass of wine, a roast chestnut, a wretched
little brazier, the sounds of the sea...

NIKOS KAZANTZAKIS

glen greenwalt
2009

A thousand cups of wine do not suffice
when true friends meet, but half a sentence is too
much when there is no meeting of friends.

CHINESE PROVERB

Pommes
Quiche
for
extra

TOS
ED

glen greenwall
2008

Wine is bottled poetry.

ROBERT LOUIS STEVENSON

LE PICHET

LE MARCEL

glen greenwood
2009

Ah, make the most of what we yet may
spend before we too into the Dust descend;
Dust into Dust, and under Dust, to lie, sans Wine,
sans Song, sans Singer, and-sans End!

EDWARD FITZGERALD

glen greenwalt
2011

Let us have wine and women,
mirth and laughter,
sermons and soda-water the day after.

Don Juan

glen greenwalt
2009

A woman drove me to drink and I didn't even have the decency to thank her.

W. C. FIELDS

glen greenwalt
2011

Wine gives us liberty,
love takes it away.
Wine makes us princes,
love makes us beggars.

WILLIAM WYCHERLEY

glen greenwalt
2009

Quickly, bring me a beaker of wine,
so that I may wet my mind and
say something clever.

ARISTOPHANES

glen greenwalt
2000

God only made water, but man made wine.

Victor Hugo

glen greenwalt
2009

Wine cheers the sad, revives the old, inspires
the young, makes weariness forget his toil.

LORD BYRON

john greenwalt
2011

Fill ev'ry glass, for wine inspires us,
and fires us up with courage, love and joy.
Women and wine should life employ.
Is there ought else on earth desirous?

JOHN GAY

glen greenwalt
2009

Wine comes in at the mouth and loves
comes in at the eye; that's all we shall know
for truth before we grow old and die.

WILLIAM BUTLER YEATS

glen greenwalt
2009

Neither do men put new wine in old bottles.

THE GOSPEL ACCORDING TO SAINT MATTHEW 9:17

gley greenwalt
2009

How much better is love than wine.

THE SONG OF SOLOMON 4:10

LE PICHET

glen greenwalt
2009

Wine, one sip of this will bathe
the drooping spirits in delight beyond
the bliss of dreams. Be wise and taste.

JOHN MILTON

glen greenwood
2011

"Wine, madam, is God's next best gift to man."

AMBROSE BIERCE

glen greenwalt
2009

Come, come, good wine is a good
familiar creature if it be but well used.
Exclaim no more against it.

WILLIAM SHAKESPEARE

glen greenwalt
2011

It is well to remember that there are five reasons for drinking: the arrival of a friend; one's present or future thirst; the excellence of wine; or any other reason.

Latin Saying

glen greenwalt
2006

In vino veritas

PLINY THE ELDER

glen gridenwald
2009

Souls of poets dead and gone…
have ye tippled drink more fine
than mine host's Canary wine?

JOHN KEATS

He who loves not wine,
women and song remains a
fool his whole life long.

MARTIN LUTHER

Wine is made to be drunk
as women are made to be loved...

THEOPHILE MALVEZIN

glen greenwalt
2009

Drink wine, and you will sleep well...
Sleep, and you will not sin...
Avoid sin and you will be saved...
Ergo, drink wine and be saved.

MEDIEVAL GERMAN SAYING

glen greenwalt
2010

Wine Improves with Age,
the older I get, the better I like it.

ANONYMOUS

Les fromages
Fiore Sardo
a Casinca
Stilton
Delice de Bourgogne
La Coquette

glen greenwalt
2011

To take wine into your mouth is to savor a
droplet of the river of human history.

CLIFTON FADIMAN

Les Fromages
Stilton
Camembert
I. Edel de Cleron
Bûche
Berges Bosque

Les Dessert
Hazelnut parfait
Apple crumble £6
Walnut Brown
Oregon Sorbet
Chocolat Orange

frites $5 Plate du Jour

Quiche Ham
£ Leek $7

glen greenwalt
2010

Compromises are for relationships, not wine.

PLINY THE ELDER

A man will be eloquent if you
give him good wine.

RALPH WALDO EMERSON

glen greenbalt
2014

Wine is the most civilized thing in the world.

ERNEST HEMINGWAY

Stilton
Camembert

L'Edel de Cleron

Bûche
Tomme de Fédou

glen greenwalt
2010

Come quickly, I am tasting the stars!

ATTRIBUTED TO DOM PERIGNON, 1638-1714,
ON HIS FIRST SIP OF CHAMPAGNE.

glengreenwelt
2010

The discovery of a wine is of greater moment
than the discovery of a constellation.
The universe is too full of stars.

BENJAMIN FRANKLIN

glen glechwald
2011

The smell of wine, oh how much more delicate,
cheerful, gratifying, celestial, and delicious
it is than that of oil.

FRANÇOIS RABELAIS

glen greenwalt
2010

Your words are my food, your breath my wine.
You are everything to me.

Sarah Bernhardt

Wine makes daily living easier, less hurried,
with fewer tensions and more tolerance.

BENJAMIN FRANKLIN

glen greenwalt
2011

The soft extractive note of an aged cork being withdrawn has the sound of a man opening his heart.

WILLIAM S. BENWELL

Les fromages
Stilton
Camembert
Saint Nectaire
Bleu du Larzac
Bûche

glen offenwalt
2010

Wine has lit up for me the pages
of literature, and revealed in life romance
lurking in the commonplace.

<small>Duff Coper</small>

glen greenwalt
2010

What I like to drink most is wine
that belongs to others.

DIOGENES

glen greenwalt
2010

Wine gives great pleasure, and every
pleasure is itself a good.

WILLIAM MAKEPEACE THACKERAY

glen greenwalt
2011

Drink to me only with thine eyes,
And I will pledge with mine;
Or leave a kiss but in the cup,
And I'll not look for wine.

BEN JONSON

glen greenwalt
2010

The Spirit of Wine sang in my glass,
and I listened with love to his odorous music,
his flushed and magnificent song.

WILLIAM ERNEST HENLEY

sert s $6
• Chocolate Gateau
• Pineapple Sorbet
chaud

glen greenwalt
2010

They are not long, the days of wine and roses.

ERNEST DOWSON

NO MINORS

glen greenwalt
2010

A bottle of wine begs to be shared;
I have never met a miserly wine lover.

CLIFTON FADIMAN

glen greenwalt
2010

Johann Wolfgang Goethe, the German poet, once was asked, which three things he would take to an island. He stated, "Poetry, a beautiful woman, and enough bottles of the world's finest wines to survive this dry period." Then he was asked what he would leave back first, if allowed only two things. He replied, "The poetry." When then asked if only allowed one thing, Goethe thought for a moment, then answered: "It depends on the vintage…"

Anonymous

glen greenwalt
2010

Acknowledgements

I would like to thank my teachers at the New York Academy of Art who taught me the rules of proportions and the construction of a beautiful form. Martha Mason, who through her own drawings taught me the beauty and energy of scribbling. Karen Fields, who watching me draw in a coffee shop, first suggested that my sketches should be published alongside quotations about coffee.

Helen Zimmermann, my agent, who believed in my project and transformed the idea I had for a regional book on Saturday mornings in my local coffee shop into three books, Morning Coffee, Afternoon Tea, and Evening Wine. Without her perseverance, as well as that of Carl Lennertz, this project would never have found a home with the wonderful people at Delphinium Books who made this dream come true. Thank you to Kathleen Servidio at HarperCollins for a beautiful book design.

Finally, I would like to thank the people who encouraged me throughout this project: my parents, Don and Rose Greenwalt; my sister Linda Tonsberg; my children, Natascha and Gavin, who are each successful artists in their own right; Dan Lamberton and Ron Jolliffe, who listened to hours of my worries; and Elena Mezisko, who not only encouraged me in this project, but added sparkle to my life.

About the Author

GLEN G. GREENWALT holds a PhD from Vanderbilt University and graduated Cum Laude from the New York Academy of Art. He has been teaching for over 20 years, currently as Adjunct Professor of Humanities at Shasta College in California.

The drawings in the three books grew out of studied observations of people who come together for social contact at coffee houses, tea rooms, and bistros. His quest was to explore and share this core experience of life through his drawings and the quotes he selected.